# One Rehearsal WONDERS Vol. 4

## ALMOST INSTANT ANTHEMS FOR ADVENT AND CHRISTMAS

To access OBBLIGATO PDFs, go to:
**www.halleonard.com/mylibrary**

Enter Code
4468-7682-2381-3469

T0066175

ISBN 978-1-4950-6188-2

# SHAWNEE ♪ PRESS

### EXCLUSIVELY DISTRIBUTED BY

## HAL•LEONARD®
### CORPORATION

7777 W. BLUEMOUND RD. P.O. BOX 13819 MILWAUKEE, WI 53213

In Australia Contact:
Hal Leonard Austraila Pty. Ltd.
4 Lentara Court
Cheltenham, Victoria, 3192 Australia
Email: ausadmin@halleonard.com.au

Visit Hal Leonard Online at
**www.halleonard.com**

Visit Shawnee Press Online at
**www.shawneepress.com**

2

# IMMANUEL, GOD WITH US

for S.A.T.B. voices, accompanied

Words by
J. PAUL WILLIAMS (ASCAP)

Music by
MICHAEL BARRETT (BMI)
*Incorporating tune:*
**HYMN OF JOY**

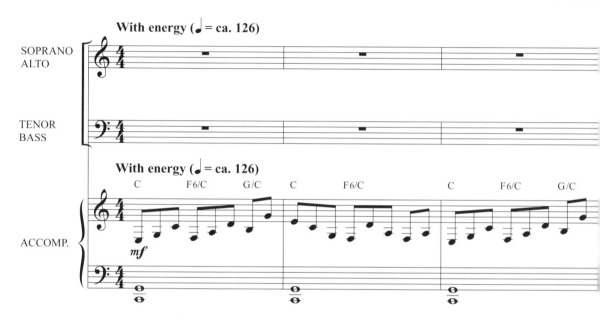

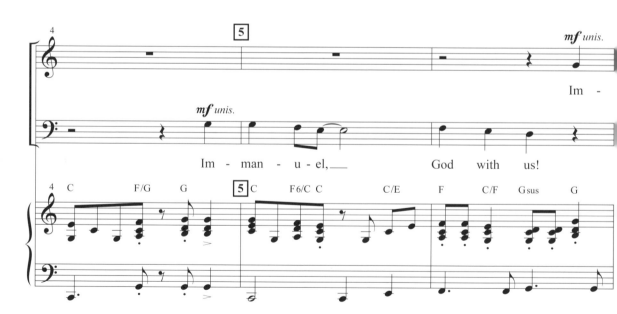

2

cho - sen One. Im - man - u - el,___ the prom - ised Son of

Is - ra - el.___  O come, Im - man - u - el.___

He will come to a low - ly man - ger in the

6

8

Come, Thou long - ex - pect - ed

Je - sus. Come, and set Thy

\* Tune: HYMN OF JOY, Ludwig van Beethoven, 1770-1827
 Words: Charles Wesley, 1707-1788, adapted by J. P. W.

10

12

# COME, JESUS, PRINCE OF PEACE

for S.A.B. voices, accompanied, with opt. violin*

*Arranged by*
BRAD NIX (ASCAP)

*Words and Music by*
DIANE HANNIBAL (ASCAP)

* Part for Violin available as a digital download
www.halleonard.com/mylibrary

14

come, O come, Em - man - u - el, we a -

wait___ Your birth.

VIOLIN

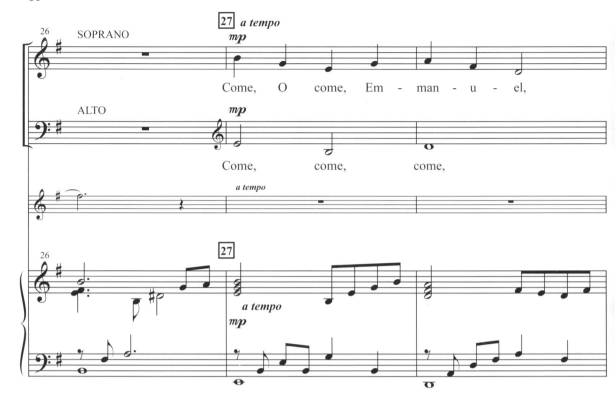

man - u - el, King with - out a crown.

Je - sus, Prince of Peace, come to guide our

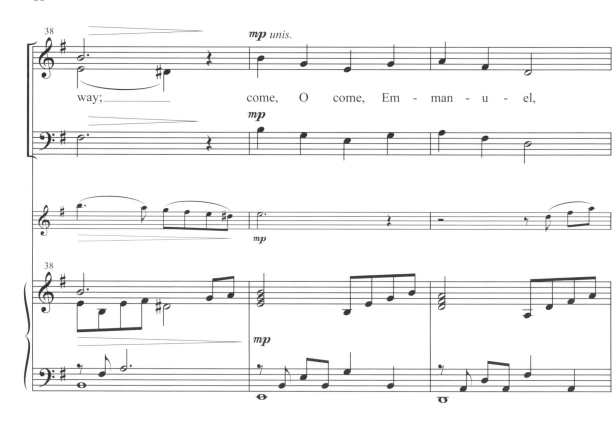

way;_____ come, O come, Em - man - u - el,

live in us____ to - day.

Come, O come, Em-
*Je - sus, Child of

man - u - el, Branch of Jes - se's tree.
Beth - le - hem, live in us to - day.

gen - tle as a dove;____ come, O come, Em -
*Sav - ior of us all,____ Je - sus, Child of*

man - u - el, Mes - sen - ger____ of
*Beth - le - hem, born in cat - tle*

*Tune: VENI EMMANUEL, 15th century Plainsong
 Words: Latin hymn, translation by John M. Neale (1818-1866)

come to thee, O Is - ra - el!

24

# AFRICAN ALLELUIA

for 2-Part mixed voices, (opt. S.A.B.), accompanied, with opt. percussion*

*Words and Music by*
BENJAMIN HARLAN (ASCAP)
*Based on a*
Kenyan Folk Melody

* Part for Percussion (triangle, shaker, congas) available as a digital download
www.halleonard.com/mylibrary

** L.H. of piano may be doubled by Electric Bass.
† R.H. of piano is optional through m. 25.
†† *loo-wee-yah* throughout

28

Sing al - le - lu - ia, Christ is born!

Sing al - le - lu - i - a!

Al - le - lu, Christ is born!

Al - le - lu, \_\_\_\_ al - le - lu - ia!

Christ is born \_\_\_\_ in Beth - le - hem!

Al - le - lu, \_\_\_\_ al - le - lu - ia!

**30**

Christ is born ___ in Beth - le - hem!

triangle only

34

Christ is born____ in Beth - le - hem!

Al - le - lu,____ al - le - lu - ia!

Christ is born____ in Beth - le - hem!

# AND GLORY SHONE AROUND

for S.A.B. voices, accompanied, with opt. handbells*

*Words by*
NAHUM TATE (1652-1715)

*Music by*
DIANE HANNIBAL (ASCAP)
*Arranged by* JON PAIGE (BMI)

* Part for Handbells (3 oct.) available as a digital download
www.halleonard.com/mylibrary

ground, the an - gel of the Lord came down and

glo - ry shone a - round, the an - gel of the

Lord came down and glo - ry shone a - round.

# A STAR, A SONG, A SIGN

for S.A.B. voices, accompanied, with opt. flute*

*Words by*
JON PAIGE (BMI)

*Music by*
BRAD NIX (ASCAP)

* Part for Flute available as a digital download
www.halleonard.com/mylibrary

44

sky.    There's a moth - er's    deep prayer and    a___    ba - by's low

cry.    And the star    rains    its___    fire    while the___    beau - ti - ful

sing, for the man-ger of Beth - le - hem cra - dles a

for the man-ger of Beth - le - hem cra - dles a

King. Now peo - ple, look

grate - ful with ju - bi - lant praise, for Je - sus is

*rit.*     *a tempo*     *rit.*

com - ing, pre - pare ye___ the way.

com - ing, pre - pare ye the way.

# A CARIBBEAN NOEL

for S.A.B. voices, accompanied, with opt. maracas*

*Words and Music by*
SHAYLA L. BLAKE (ASCAP)
*Based on a* Puerto Rican melody

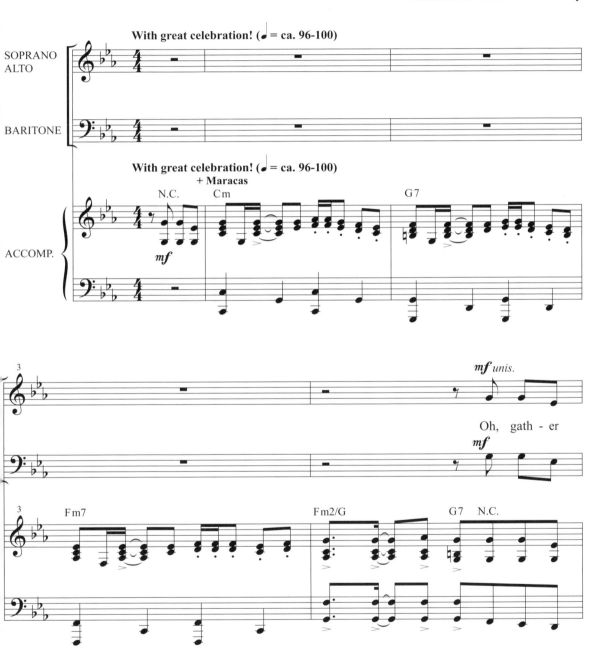

* Part for Maracas available as a digital download
www.halleonard.com/mylibrary

54

11
boy child came that bless - ed Christ - mas Day!
11
Cm/G
G7
Cm
N.C.
13
14
mf
In Beth - le - hem, a nois - y, crowd - ed
13
Fm2/G
G7
N.C.
14
Cm
mf
15
cit - y, Jo - seph could find no room, no place for them to
15
G7

60

ONE REHEARSAL WONDERS, Vol. 4 - Advent and Christmas

62

Lyrics:

sto - ry, how Ma - ry's boy child came that blessed, that bless - ed Christ - mas Day! Blessed day! That bless - ed, bless - ed Christ - mas Day!

# A TIME FOR ADVENT

for 2-Part mixed voices, accompanied

*Words and Music by*
**STEWART HARRIS (BMI)**

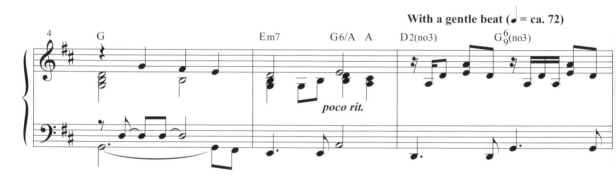

\* Tune: ES IST EIN ROS'; German Carol, 15th Century

66

wor - ship and praise. This is a mo - ment to seek His glo - ry.
Dsus2/4 D Em7 A F♯m7 Bm7
This is the dawn - ing of grace.
Em7 Asus
cresc. poco a poco
f
Let ev - 'ry land pro-claim it, let
B♭sus B♭
37
E♭2(no3) A♭6/9(no3)
f

70

# WAY DOWN YONDER IN BETHLEHEM

for S.A.B. voices, accompanied

*Words and Music by*
MICHAEL BARRETT (BMI)

72

boy. An - gels sing - ing, prais - es ring - ing, wise men bring - ing their gifts from far a - way._____ Shep - herds

praise - ing, star - light blaz - ing, it's so a - maz - ing, our King is born to - day, born to - day.

OPTIONAL DESCANT
*(solo or small group)*

78

# SEE AMID THE WINTER'S SNOW

### for S.A.B. voices, accompanied, with opt. congregational refrain*

*Words by*
EDWARD CASWALL (1814-1878)

*Music b*
JOHN GOSS (1800-1880
*Tune:* HUMILIT*
*Arranged by* DAVID LANTZ III (ASCA

* Part for Congregation available as a digital download
www.halleonard.com/mylibrary

82

Christ is born in Beth - le - hem.

Say, you ho - ly shep - herds, say,

tell    your    joy - ful    news    to - day.

Why    have    you    now    left    your    sheep

on    the    lone - ly    moun - tain    steep?

*cresc.*

lem:    Christ    is    born    in    Beth    -    le    -

hem.

**molto rit.**
SOPRANO

ALTO, BARITONE *and* CONGREGATION *(opt.)*    *f* *unis.*

**61**    **More broadly than Tempo I**    *f*

"As        we    watched        at

"As        we    watched        at

**61**    **More broadly than Tempo I**

**molto rit.**    *f*

*cresc.*

# GO, TELL IT ON THE MOUNTAIN

for 2-Part mixed voices, accompanied

rses by
OHN W. WORK, JR. (1872-1925)

African-American Spiritual
*Arranged by*
GARY LANIER

92

**96**

ONE REHEARSAL WONDERS, Vol. 4 - Advent and Christm